John Rutter

Anthems

T0088394

11 anthems for mixed voices

Contents

Two unaccompanied prayers
God be in my head 2
A Prayer of Saint Patrick 4

Four accompanied anthems
All things bright and beautiful 6
For the beauty of the earth 12
I will sing with the spirit 23
Look at the world 31

Four blessings
Go forth into the world in peace 42
A Clare Benediction 46
The Lord bless you and keep you 51
The peace of God 56

A Choral Amen 62

The accompanied items are all available in versions with orchestra. Instrumentation is shown at the foot of the relevant first pages. Full scores and instrumental parts are available on hire from the publisher.

MUSIC DEPARTMENT
OXFORD
UNIVERSITY PRESS

God be in my head

Words from the Sarum Primer

JOHN RUTTER

© Oxford University Press, Inc. 1970 and 2003. Assigned to Oxford University Press 2010. Photocopying this copyright material is ILLEGAL

12
speak - - - - ing.
mf
in my mouth and in my
speak - - - - ing.
speak - - - - ing.
mouth and
mf
16
p
God be in mine heart and in my
p
Poco meno mosso
19
pp
think - ing. God be at my end
pp
22
pp
rit.
ppp
and in my de - part - - - ing.
pp
ppp

A Prayer of Saint Patrick

Words from
Saint Patrick's Breastplate (5th century)
Translated by Mrs C. F. Alexander (1823–95)

JOHN RUTTER

© Oxford University Press, Inc. 1970 and 2003. Assigned to Oxford University Press 2010. Photocopying this copyright material is ILLEGAL

10
Christ be - neath me,
cresc.
mf
Christ be - neath me, Christ in qui - et, Christ in dan - ger,
cresc.
mf

13
cresc.
f
mf dim.
Christ in hearts of all that love me, Christ in mouth of friend and
cresc.
Christ in
f
mf dim.

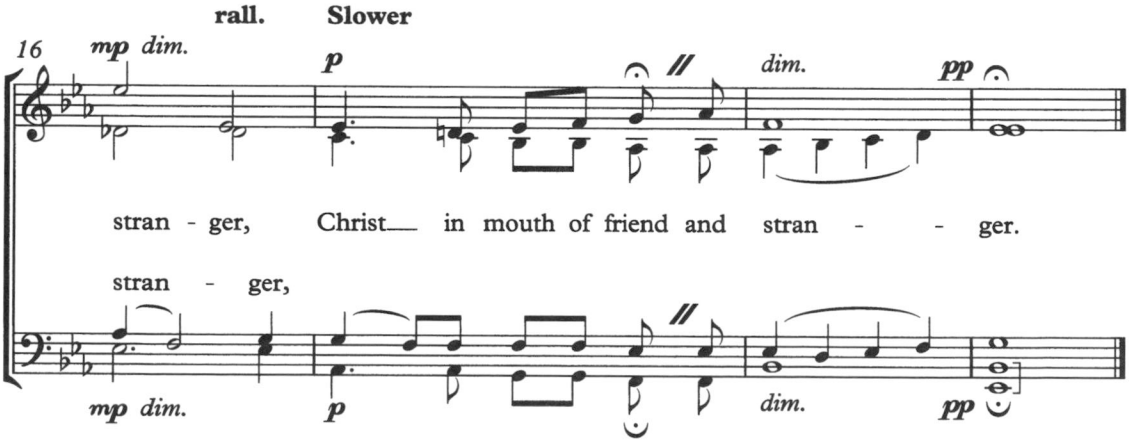
rall. Slower
16
mp dim.
p
dim.
pp
stran - ger, Christ in mouth of friend and stran - - ger.
stran - ger,
mp dim.
p
dim.
pp

All things bright and beautiful

Words by Mrs C. F. Alexander (1823–95)

JOHN RUTTER

Also available for unison voices, with optional second part (U162). Instrumentation: 2fl, 2ob, 2cl, bsn, 2hn, perc, hp, str

© Oxford University Press 1983 and 2003. Photocopying this copyright material is ILLEGAL.

*or hum, at conductor's discretion

29
Lord God made them all.
Lord God made them all.
T.
B.
Ah
The
mf
mf
f dolce
mf
B
33
pur - ple - head - ed moun - tain, The riv - er run - ning by, The
unis.
B
Ped. * Ped. * Ped. *
37
S. and A.
unis. mp
The
sun - set and the morn - ing, That bright - ens up the sky;
mp

41
(S. and A.)
cold wind in the win - ter, The plea - sant sum - mer sun, The
mp
Ped.
Ped.
sim.
45
cresc.
mf
poco rit.
ripe fruits in the gar - den, He made them ev - 'ry one:
cresc.
mf
poco rit.
cresc.
mf
Ped.
Ped.
49
C a tempo
(mf)
All things bright and beau-ti - ful, All crea-tures great and small,
(mf)
C a tempo
(mf)

53
All things wise and won - der-ful, The Lord God made them all.
57
cresc.
He gave us eyes to see them, And lips that we might tell How
f
cresc.
f
cresc.
f
61
all things well.
great is God Al - might - y, Who has made all things well.

65
D
(f)
great and
All things bright and beau-ti-ful, All crea-tures great and small,
(f)
great and
D
(f)
Ped.
sim.
69
rall.
mp
All things wise and won-der-ful,
The
mp
rall.
l.h.
mf dim.
mp
73
dim.
a tempo
p
Lord God made them all.
dim.
p
a tempo
dim.
p
Ped.
76
rall.
pp
Ped.
Ped.

for Rosemary Heffley and the Texas Choral Directors' Association

For the beauty of the earth

Words by F. S. Pierpoint (1835–1917)

JOHN RUTTER

Also available in a two-part version (SS or SA) (T113). Instrumentation: 2fl, ob, 2cl, bsn, 2hn, perc, hp, str

© Oxford University Press 1980 and 2003. Photocopying this copyright material is ILLEGAL.

16
For the love which from our birth
20
O - ver and a - round us lies, o - ver and a -
23
mf
-round us lies: Lord of all, to thee we
mf
27
mp
raise This our joy - ful hymn of
mp

31
praise.
35
A
SOPRANO
mf
ALTO
2. For the beau - ty of each hour
TENOR
BASS
mf
A
mf
39
Hill and
Of the day and of the night,
Hill and

43
S.
vale and tree and flower, Sun and moon and
A.
Hill and vale and tree and flower, Sun and moon and
T.
Hill and vale and tree and flower,
B.
vale and tree and flower,
47
stars of light: Lord of
stars of light: Lord of
Sun and moon and stars of light: Lord of
Sun and moon and stars of light: Lord of
3
cresc.

51
f
all, to thee we raise
3
all, to thee we raise
all, to thee we raise
all, to thee we raise
55
mf
This our joy - ful hymn of praise.
This our hymn of praise.
This our joy - ful hymn of praise.
This our hymn of praise.
mp
espress.
Ped.
*

59
B
(T. and B.)
unis.
mp espress.
3. For the joy of hu - man
B
p dolce
Ped.
63
(S. and A.)
unis.
p
3. For the joy of love,
love,
Bro - ther, sis - ter, pa - rent,
67
Bro - ther, sis - ter, pa - rent, child, Friends on earth,
child,
Friends on earth,
and friends a -

71
(p)
and friends a - bove,
For all
- bove,
For all gen - tle thoughts and mild,
74
gen - tle thoughts and mild:
For all gen - tle thoughts and mild:
Lord of
77
mf
Lord of all,
to thee we raise
mf
all, to thee we raise
mf

81
unis. p
Our joy-ful hymn of praise.
mp
This our joy - ful hymn of praise.
mp
cresc.
85
C ALL VOICES
unis. f
4. For each per - fect gift of thine
f
89
SOPRANOS
To our race so free - ly giv - en,
ALTOS, TENORS, BASSES
To our race so free - ly giv - en,
mf
Gra - ces
mf

93
mf
Gra - ces hu -man and di - vine,
hu - - - - - man and di - vine,
96
Ah
Flow'rs of earth and buds of heav'n, Flow'rs of earth and
99
cresc.
S.
f
Ah
A.
Lord of all, to
cresc.
T.
buds of heav'n,
B.
f
cresc.
f

102
S.
thee we raise
A.
thee we raise
T.
thee we raise
B.
thee we raise
105
D (♪ = ♪)
mf
This our joy - ful hymn of praise,
This our joy - ful hymn of praise,
This our joy - ful hymn of praise,
This our joy - ful hymn of praise,
D (♪ = ♪)
mf

111
rall.
(rallentando al fine)
p
This our joy - ful hymn of praise.
p
our hymn of praise.
p
our hymn of praise.
p
our hymn of praise.
rall.
(rallentando al fine)
dim.
p
(p)
115
molto rall.

for the Royal School of Church Music

I will sing with the spirit

I Corinthians 14, v.15

JOHN RUTTER

Also available for 2-part voices (E162). Instrumentation: 2fl, ob, 2cl, bsn, 2hn, str

© Oxford University Press 1994 and 2003. Photocopying this copyright material is ILLEGAL.

13
-lu - ia, al - le - lu - ia, al-le - lu - ia, al - le - lu - ia, al-le-
(Sw.)
Sw.
17
cresc.
-lu - ia, al-le - lu - ia, al-le - lu - - ia:
f dolce
SOPRANOS and ALTOS unis. mf
I will
TENORS and BASSES unis.
mf
Ch. 8′ + 2′
cresc.
mf
Ped. (with 16′)
21
sing with the spi - - rit,
I will

25
sing with the spi - - rit: al-le-
29
mp
-lu - ia, al - le - lu - ia, al-le - lu - ia, al - le - lu - ia, al-le-
mp
33
cresc.
mf cresc.
f dolce
-lu - ia, al-le - lu - ia, al-le - lu - - ia, al - le - lu - -
cresc.
mf cresc.
f dolce
Sw.
mp
cresc.
mf

37
mf
- ia.
mf
mp
Ch.
41
SOPRANOS
mp dolce e legato
And I will sing with the un - der - stand - ing al - so: al-le-
Ch. Fl.
Sw. or Ch.
p
Man.
46
ALTOS
mf dolce e legato
-lu - ia, al - le - lu - - - ia:
And I will sing with the un - der -
Sw.
mp
Ped.

50
(ALTOS)
mp
-stand - - ing al - so: al - le - lu - ia, al - le - lu - - -
54
-ia:
S.
mf
al - le-
A.
And I will sing with the un - der - stand - - ing al - so:
al - le-
T.
B.
mp dolce e legato
mf
cresc.
58
-lu - ia,
cresc.
allarg.
f
a tempo
-lu - ia, al - le - lu - ia, al - le - lu - - - ia.
cresc.
f
allarg.
a tempo
(Sw.)
mf
cresc.
f
mf
Gt. or Ch.

62
cresc.
f
66
f
(S.)
I will sing with the spi - - rit, sing
(A.)
I will sing with the spi - - rit,
unis.
f
Ch. or Sw.
mf
Sw.
70
al - le - lu - ia, Sing al - le - lu - ia
I will sing with the spi - - rit:
(T.)
(B.)

74
al-le - lu - ia, al - le - lu - ia, al-le - lu - ia, al - le -

78
mp
cresc.
rallentando
mf
-lu - ia, al-le - lu - ia, al-le - lu - ia, al-le - lu - ia,
mp
cresc.
mf
rallentando
dim.
mp
cresc.
mf

82
a tempo, poco meno mosso (♩ = 108)
dim.
mp
p
al - le - lu - - ia,
al-le - lu - ia,
dim.
mp
p
a tempo, poco meno mosso (♩ = 108)
Sw.
mp
dim.
p
Ch. or Sw.
Ped. (with 16′)

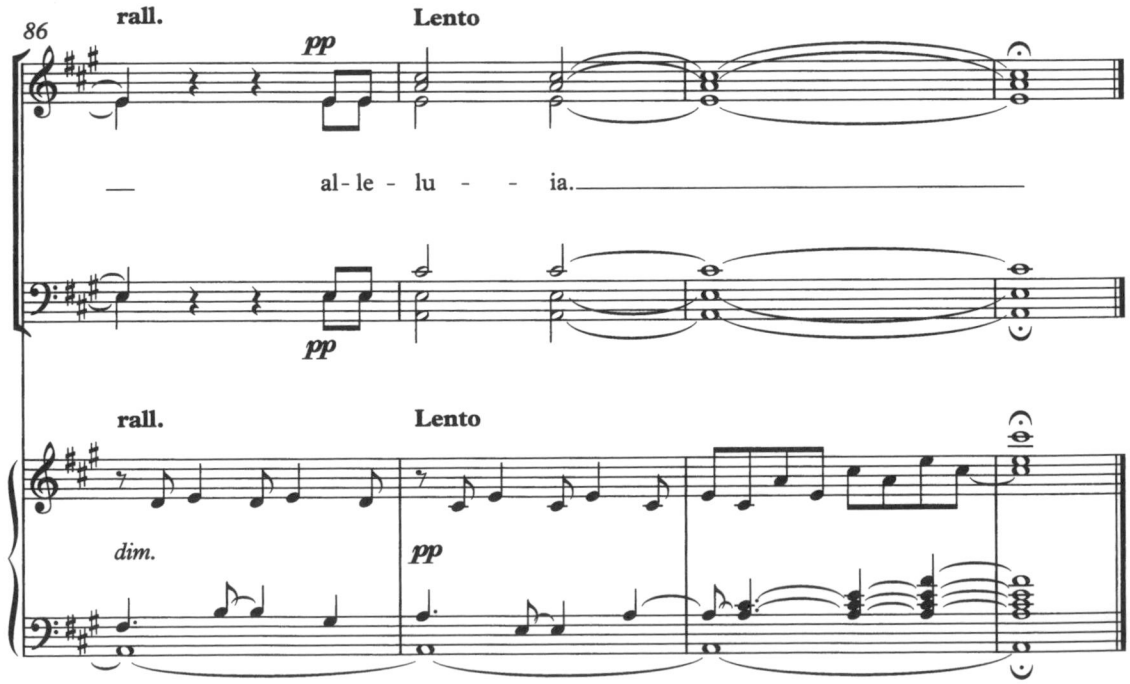
86
rall.
pp
Lento
al-le - lu - - ia.
pp
rall.
Lento
dim.
pp

in celebration of the 70th anniversary of the Council for the Protection of Rural England

Look at the world

for children's choir (unison) and/or mixed choir (SATB)

Words and music by
JOHN RUTTER

*The accompaniment is more suitable for piano, but it can be played on the organ.

Instrumentation: 2fl, ob, 2cl, bsn, 2hn, hp, str

© Oxford University Press 1996 and 2003. Photocopying this copyright material is ILLEGAL.

17
Look at the world: so ma-ny joys and won-ders,

21
So ma-ny mi - ra - cles a - long our way.

A
SOPRANOS (and CHILDREN)
25
mf
ALTOS
Praise to thee, O Lord, for all cre - - a - tion,
TENORS
mf
BASSES
mf
(Ped.)

29
Give us thank - ful hearts, that we may see:
33
dim.
All the gifts we share, and ev - 'ry bless - ing,
dim.
dim.
37
mp
All things come of thee.
mp
mp
cresc.

41
B
CHILDREN (or SOPRANOS and ALTOS)
mf
2. Look at the earth
mf
45
bring-ing forth fruit and flow - er; Look at the sky,— the
49
(TENORS and BASSES)
mf
sun-shine and the rain; Look at the hills,
53
(SOPRANOS and ALTOS)
look at the trees and moun - tains, Val - ley and

56
flow - ing ri - ver, field and plain:
C
59
f
Praise to thee, O Lord, for all cre - - a - tion,
f
f
63
Give us thank - ful hearts, that we may see:

67
mf
dim.
All the gifts we share, and ev - 'ry bless - ing,
mf
dim.
mf
dim.
71
mp
All things come of thee.
mp
mp
mf
75
D
CHILDREN (or TENORS and BASSES)
mp legato
3. Think of the spring,
mp legato

79
think of the warmth of sum-mer Bring-ing the har-vest be -
83
-fore the win - ter's cold. Ev - 'ry - thing
86
grows, ev-'ry-thing has a sea - son, Till it is
90
ga - thered to the Fa - ther's fold:

* Small notes in the accompaniment should be played for unison performances (without A. T. B. singers).

108
F
ALL VOICES f
4. Ev-'ry good
(cresc.)
f
112
gift, all that we need and che - rish
115
Comes from the Lord in to - ken of his love;
119
(TENORS and BASSES)
mf
We are his hands, stew-ards of all his boun - ty;
mf

123
(SOPRANOS and ALTOS)
mf
cresc.
His is the earth, and his the heav'ns a - bove:
cresc.
127
G
f
Praise to thee, O Lord, for all cre - a - tion,
f
f
131
dim.
Give us thank - ful hearts, that we may see:
dim.
dim.

135
mf
dim.
All the gifts we share, and ev - 'ry bless - ing,
mf
dim.
mf
dim.
139
mp
All things come of thee,
mp
mp
dim.
143
rall. al fine
p
all things come of thee.
p
rall. al fine
p

for Tim Brown and the choir of Clare College, Cambridge

Go forth into the world in peace

Words from the
Book of Common Prayer (1928)

JOHN RUTTER

Instrumentation: strings

© Oxford University Press 1988 and 2003. Photocopying this copyright material is ILLEGAL.

8
mp
forth in - to the world in peace; be of good cou - rage,
be of good
mp
Ped.
11
cou - rage;
hold fast that which is good;
unis.
mp
3
14
A.
p
ren - der to no one e - vil for e - vil;
strength - en the faint -
T.
p
3
B.
p

17
mp
sup - port the weak;
mp
p cresc.
mp
help— the af -
- heart - ed;
sup - port the weak;
p cresc.
mp
cresc.
mp
21
mf cresc.
-flict - ed;
hon - our all peo - ple;
love and serve the
mp cresc.
mf cresc.
cresc.
mf cresc.
25
f dolce
Lord, re - joi - cing in the pow'r of the Ho - ly Spi - rit.
And the
f dolce
mp
f dolce
mp

28
bless - ing of God Al - migh - ty, the Fa - ther, the Son and the
31
mp
poco cresc.
mf
be up - on you, and re - main with you for e - -
Ho - ly Ghost,
(mp)
poco cresc.
mf
p
35
p
rall.
p
molto
pp
A - - - - men.
-ver. A - - - men, a - - - - men.
p
mp
p
pp
A - - - men, a - - - men.
rall.
molto
mp
p
pp

for Clare College, Cambridge

A Clare Benediction

Words and music by
JOHN RUTTER

Also available for SATB unaccompanied (E166), for SSA (W138), and for unison or two-part voices (U172)
Instrumentation: 2fl, ob, 2cl, bsn, 2hn, hp, str

© Oxford University Press 1998 and 2003. Photocopying this copyright material is ILLEGAL.

21
A
cresc.
mf
sleep, may his an - gels watch o-ver you; when you wake, may he
cresc.
mf
26
SOPRANOS
and TENORS
mf cresc.
fill you with his grace: May you love him and
30
f ma dolce
dim.
SOPRANOS
and ALTOS
mp
serve him all your days, Then in hea - ven may you
dim.
mp
35
see his face.
Ch.

40
S.
A.
p dolce
B
mp
May the Lord show his mer - cy up - on you; may the
T.
B.
p dolce
B
Sw.
mp
p
45
light of his pre-sence be your guide: May he guard
poco cresc.
mp
Ch.
50
you and up - hold you; may his spi - rit be ev-er by your
Sw.

55
C
p
side.
Ah
(mp)
When you sleep, may his an - gels watch
C
59
cresc.
ah
cresc.
mf
o - ver you;
when you wake, may he fill you with his
cresc.
mf
63
mf
cresc.
f
May you love him and serve him
grace:
cresc.
f
Ch. or Sw.
cresc.
f

poco rall.
dim.
a tempo
Then in hea - ven may you see
mp
all your days,
A.
T.
B.
Hum
poco rall.
dim.
a tempo
mp
Sw.
p
Man.
his face,
may you
S.
A.
T.
B.
Then in hea - ven
may you
Ped.
rall.
poco meno mosso
rit.
see his face,
dim.
p
pp
may you see his face, may you see his face.
see his face, see his face.
Ch.

in memoriam Edward T. Chapman

The Lord bless you and keep you

Numbers 6, v.24

JOHN RUTTER

Also available for SA (T119). Instrumentation: strings

© Oxford University Press 1981 and 2003. Photocopying this copyright material is ILLEGAL.

10
S.
p dolce sempre
you.
A.
The Lord bless you and keep you: The
T.
B.
p dolce sempre
13
mp
Lord make his face to shine up-on you, to shine up - on you and be
mp
mp
16
gra - cious,
mp cresc.
gra - - cious, and be gra - cious un - to you:
The
gra - cious
gra - - cious, and be gra - - cious un - to you:

19
mf
Lord lift up the light of his coun - te - nance up -
cresc.
mf
22
- on you,
The Lord lift up the light of his
mp cresc.
mf
mp
cresc.
mf
25
mp
and give you
coun - te - nance up - on you
mp

28
dim.
peace,
and give you peace,
p
dim.
dim.
p
dim.
31
pp
p
and give you peace,
and give you
pp
p
pp
34
poco rit.
a tempo
peace.
peace.
A - - - - - men,
mp
poco rit.
a tempo
(Ch.)
cresc.
mp

37
S.
A.
T.
B.
mf
f
mf
a - - - - men, a - - - - men, a -
a - - men, a - - men, a - men, a - men,
a - - - - men, a - - men,
a - men, a - men, a - - - - - -
cresc.
Sw.
mf cresc.
41
mp
rall.
molto rall.
p dim.
pp
men, a - men, a - men, a - - - men.
a - - men, a - - - - men, a - - men.
a - - - men, a - - - - men, a - - - men.
-men, a - men, a - - - - - men.
mf dim.
p
dim.

for Bishop Thomas McMahon and the people of the Diocese of Brentwood

The peace of God

Book of Common Prayer (1662)
based on Philippians 4, v.7

JOHN RUTTER

Also available for SSA (W110). Instrumentation: strings

© Oxford University Press 1991 and 2003. Photocopying this copyright material is ILLEGAL.

13
S. p dolce
know - ledge and love of God, and of his Son Je - sus Christ our Lord:
A.
The
T.
B.
p dolce
p
17
A
peace of God, which pass - eth all un - der - stand - ing,
A
21
mp
cresc.
mf
keep your hearts and minds, keep your hearts and minds in the
mp
cresc.
mf
mp
cresc.

25
f dolce
Son Je - sus Christ
know-ledge and love of God, and of his Son Je - sus Christ our
Son Je - sus
f dolce
mf
f
30
mf
B
Lord:
unis.
mp dolce cantabile
mf
and the bless - ing of God Al -
B
mf
mp
34
- migh - ty, the Fa - ther, the Son, and the

38
S.
p
cresc.
mp
be a - mongst you, be a -
A.
p
cresc.
mp
be a - mongst you, be a -
T.
p
cresc.
mp
Ho - ly Ghost, be a - mongst you, be a -
B.
p
cresc.
mp
Ho - ly Ghost, be a - mongst you, be a -
p
cresc.
mp
42
cresc.
mf
cresc.
-mongst you, be a - mongst you and re - main with you
cresc.
mf
cresc.
-mongst you, be a - mongst you and re - main with you
cresc.
mf
cresc.
-mongst you, be a - mongst you and re - main with you
cresc.
mf
cresc.
-mongst you, be a - mongst you and re - main with you
cresc.
mf
cresc.

C
46
f
mp dolce e legato
al - ways.
A - - - - - men,
f
mp
dolce e legato
al - - - ways.
A - - - - - - -
f
mp
mp dolce e legato
al - - ways.
A - -
f
mp
al - - ways.
A - - - - - - - -
C
f
mp
51
poco rit.
p
a - - men, a - - men,
p
- men, a - - - - - - men,
p
- - - men, a - - men,
p
-men, a - - - - - men, a - - - men,
poco rit.
p

D
a tempo
56
mp cresc.
a - - -
mp cresc.
a - - -
p cresc.
mp cresc.
a - - - men,
a - - -
cresc.
mp cresc.
a - - - men,
a - - - men,
a - - -
D
a tempo
cresc.
mp cresc.
61
mf
mp
dim.
rall.
pp
-men, a - - - men, a - - men, a - men, a - men.
mf
mp
dim.
pp
-men, a - - - - men, a - - men, a - - men.
mf
mp dim.
pp
-men, a - - - men, a - men, a - - men.
mf
mp dim.
pp
-men, a - - - men, a - - - - - men.
rall.
mf
mp dim.
pp

A Choral Amen

JOHN RUTTER

© Oxford University Press 1981 and 2003. Photocopying this copyright material is ILLEGAL.

6
(cresc.)
f dolce
dim.
men, a men,
S.
(cresc.)
f dolce
dim.
a men, a men, a-
p cresc.
f dolce
dim.
a men, a men, a men,
A.
(cresc.)
f dolce
dim.
men, a men, a men, a-
f dolce
dim.
men, a men, a men,
T.
f dolce
dim.
men, A men, a-
(cresc.)
f dolce
dim.
men, a men, a men, a-
B.
(cresc.)
f dolce
dim.
men, a men,
f
dim.

Printed by Halstan